Sarah Bachelard

*Experiencing God in a Time of Crisis*

*Revised by Liam Kelly*

**CONVIVIUM**PRESS

MEDITATIO

2012

*Experiencing God in a Time of Crisis*

© Sarah Bachelard

© Convivium Press 2012
All rights reserved
For the English Edition

http://www.conviviumpress.com
sales@conviviumpress.com
convivium@conviviumpress.com

7661 NW 68th St, Suite 108,
Miami, Florida 33166. USA.
Phone: +1 (305) 8890489
Fax: +1 (305) 8875463

Edited by Rafael Luciani
Revised by Liam Kelly
Designed by Eduardo Chumaceiro d'E
Series: *Meditatio*

ISBN: 978-1-934996-32-4

Printed in Colombia
Impreso en Colombia
D'VINNI, S.A.

Convivium Press
Miami, 2012

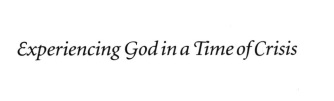

*Experiencing God in a Time of Crisis*

# Contents

1

*Experiencing God* PAGE 9

1. *First, God* PAGE 14
2. *So, Experience* PAGE 23
3. *Experiencing God* PAGE 28
4. *Being called* PAGE 30
5. *Self-criticism* PAGE 37
6. *Conclusion* PAGE 41


2

*Collapsing Stories* PAGE 43

1. *A Time of Crisis* PAGE 45
2. *God and Crisis* PAGE 51
3. *The Wayless Way* PAGE 60
4. *The Surrender of Friday* PAGE 62
5. *The Waiting of Saturday* PAGE 67
6. *The Gift of Sunday* PAGE 71
7. *Conclusion* PAGE 75

### 3
### *Living Contemplative in a Time of Crisis* PAGE 79

1. *Grace* PAGE 81
2. *Living Until We Die* PAGE 91
3. *Living in the Tragic Gap* PAGE 99
4. *Beyond Being Right* PAGE 105
5. *Experiencing God in a Time of Crisis* PAGE 111

# *Experiencing God*

People sometimes say to believers who are in crisis: «Still, your faith must be a comfort to you now» and I have heard believers say similarly, «I don't know how people manage if they don't believe in God». These kinds of statements have always made me a bit uneasy —although I have probably thought or said versions of them myself. They make me uneasy because they have about them a hint of false consolation, a hint that God might be being used as a shield against reality. At times they convey an air of desperate belief —no matter what happens, I cannot afford to give this up, this structure for viewing the world. It reminds me of my 7 year-old nephew, already disillusioned about the existence of Father Christmas and furious to catch his mother giving him money for one of his baby teeth in lieu of the tooth fairy. «It's not fair», he wailed piteously, «there's only the Easter bunny left!».

Of course, faith *is* a source of strength and consolation, so this is a subtle question. It is not that it is illegitimate to find through faith in God hope, strength to endure, and peace in the face of uncertainty —indeed if faith made no difference to the way in which we experience crisis, then we would have to ask what it amounts to. Nevertheless, I sometimes find myself uneasy at the way the word, the name, «God» is wielded so casually by believers —as if everyone was clear what that meant and how it helped. Recently I was at a conference where every second sentence had the word «God» or «godly» in it, and where all plans were referenced in relation to bringing about God's «kingdom». I found myself wondering what would happen if we banned the use of these words in such meetings. I wondered if in fact we would start to be clearer what we were trying to say, if we weren't allowed to insert «God» as a placeholder and, in fact, if we would discover whether we were saying anything much at all.

My topic for this series of meditations is «Experiencing God in a Time of Crisis». False gods abound in times of crisis as, relatedly, do false grabs for resolution or certainty. I want to explore, ultimately, how a contemplative knowledge and experience of God might shape our living abundantly and truthfully in and through times of fear, scarcity, loss and grief. Whether these times have their origin in some of the global crises of late capitalism, in experiences of personal suffering and loss, age-ing and death, or in the collapse of structures of meaning in the Western world, very few of us (and perhaps ironically they are the *unlucky* ones) makes it unwounded through life. What difference, if any, does «God» make? What is an authentic, as opposed to a falsely consoling, «experience of God in a time of crisis»? And, importantly for our gathering, how does a contemplative practice of prayer and presence make a difference at such times?

To discuss these questions seriously we need to do some preliminary clearing of the ground, some critical work on the concepts that we bring to the table. In this meditation, I aim to do some of that work by looking more closely at what the «experi-ence of God», or what «experiencing God» might be. What is it that we experience when we experi-ence God? How do we know that it is *God* we are experiencing? I want to engage these questions in the first instance by exploring the concepts of «God» and «experience» separately and in a bit more depth.

# First, God

∽

In a profound essay on the concept of monotheism, the English theologian James Alison has written that: «God is much more like "nothing at all" than like "one of the gods"»[1]. This is a crucial insight into the right use of the word «God» in the Judaeo-Christian tradition, and I want to unpack the background to it.

Alison notes that the claim that there is one God can be heard in two different ways. Either it can signify there is *one* God, as opposed to «two, three, or seventy-nine», in which case «one» clarifies how many gods there are. One is the number of gods. Alternatively the claim that there is one God might signify that there *is* God, as opposed to nothing, in which case, Alison says, «"one" is more like the exclamation "is!" than it is like a number»[2]. The

---

1  ALISON J., *Undergoing God: dispatches from the scene of a break-in* (London: Darton, Longman & Todd, 2006), p.18.
2  ALISON J., *Undergoing God*, p.18. Cf. Barth on the «oneness» of God.

significance of this is that if God is one among a possible set of gods, a set that just happens to be otherwise empty, then we learn in part what the word God means with reference to a general notion of gods. God is more like the gods (who happen not to exist) than anything else in the universe. On the other hand, if God just is, as opposed to «is not», then we have no prior concept of what kind of a «thing» God is. In fact, classical theology has always asserted the «no-thingness» of God —God is not one of the things in the universe, but is the condition of there being a universe at all. God is then much more like «nothing at all», «no-thing», than like one of the gods.

It might seem, in our «de-mythologising» and sophisticated world, as though we know this, and it is true I think that we do not *picture* God as a «thing» in the world. Nevertheless, there are ways other than the carving of idols to turn God into one of the gods, a player in our schemes of power and meaning. The sociological critique of religion has long argued that the word «god» often signifies nothing more than a projection of the group identity of «his» worshippers. It is nothing other than that which underwrites a group's identity over against other groups, and who is on «our side» against the wicked or the «god-forsaken» other. In a similar vein the psychological critique of religion has suggested that God is nothing more than a projection of our desire for security and approval, a cosmic and benign «father figure» who will make everything «ok». It is undeniable that these forms of construction or projection are pervasive in much contemporary talk of God.

Alison, for example, has identified the sociological use of the name «God» as a rallying call for the true community of «his» faithful followers in contexts ranging from Osama bin Laden's attempt to revivify a Muslim identity opposed to the «west», to some conservative evangelical groups defining themselves and their God through their stance on gays, to the attempt by some Catholic bishops to rally support for a church allegedly being persecuted by the godless «world» by being called to account for decades of clerical abuse[3]. In all these situations, a group is seeking to underwrite and

---

3   ALISON J., *Undergoing God*, pp.21-23.

strengthen its identity by understanding itself as a victim or potential victim of the wicked other. If it can be argued that the victimisation of the group follows from its faithfulness to the one true God, then the fervour surrounding the construction and maintenance of group boundaries is even more potent. So even if the «God» appealed to in all these cases is understood to be the only god there is, the underlying reference is to a god who is one of the gods. The underlying reference is to a god who is my god and not yours, *Gott mit uns*. Despite the use of monotheistic language, what is really going on is idolatry —god who is among the gods, rather than God who is no-thing.

I said at the beginning that I was uneasy with certain expressions which smacked of false consolation —your faith must be a comfort to you now —and I wonder if here is another instance of a *Gott mit uns* mentality. God again at human disposal— God a function of my identity or my need. And again, the point is that wherever appeal to God functions to shore up identity and righteousness over against others, or wherever God is at my disposal, then what is really at work is rightly described by the sociological or psychological analyses of religion.

So the question arises whether there is any way of speaking of or relating to the God who is more like no-thing at all than like one of the gods? Is there really God in this sense —is there really an other Other, utterly outside of and not a function of group identity and projection? In another helpful formulation, Alison has remarked that monotheism is true only as discovery. In fact, he says, «monotheism is a terrible idea, but a wonderful discovery»[4]. I take this to mean that the *idea* of one God is inevitably going to degenerate into idolatry, but that the confession that there *is* one God is a response to being addressed by that reality. Or, to put that differently, the authentic confession that there is one God, that God is, is never my idea.

What entitles us to think that the confession «God is» is true rather than a delusion or species of projection? Alison points out two things that accompany the emergence of monotheistic con-

4  ALISON J., *Undergoing God*, p.17.

fession in the Hebrew Scriptures that give evidence for its authenticity. The first is that from the outset, monotheistic confession of God leads immediately to self-criticism. Whereas the god who is a function of group identity props up a «we» against a wicked «they» and rails against the heathen «other», the one God of Israel inveighs far more severely against the «we» whose God he is. This God does not congratulate the people of Israel on their goodness and righteousness, but calls them again and again to repentance and self-criticism. This God convicts Israel again and again of idolatry and false worship. This is not just a matter of Yahweh's anger when the people turn aside to worship the Baals, but perhaps more deeply of Yahweh's anger when they treat Yahweh as one of the gods: «I desire steadfast love and not sacrifice, the knowledge of God rather than burnt offerings» (Hosea 6.6).

Second, where God is a function of group identity and sociological construction, then, as Alison puts it, the group is the «we» and «God is the more or less tokenistic "he" or "it" which backs up the group and gives it the impetus to keep up its group frontiers against the "they" on which the group is secretly dependent»[5]. But something much stranger seems to be coming about in the emerging monotheism of the Hebrew scriptures. It is that it is God, not the group, who is «I» or «we» and the group which gains its identity only in relation to this «I» that is God. The structure is inverted —rather than God being a function of the group identity, the group identity, the becoming of this people, is a function of its listening over time to the voice of God, who gives his name as «I AM». «This "I Am" is never a function of the group, but always a voice which can only be heard through self-critical listening»[6]. As a consequence, the «we» that comes into being over time in response to the call of this «I Am» is never an identity owned or securely possessed by the «we» —it is always in the process of being called into being, responsive to the one who calls.

So let me summarise. The word «God» is, as we all know, able to be filled with more or less infinite content. Much of this content is, as Feuerbach rightly said, nothing more than unreconstructed humanity writ large, some form of personal or

5   ALISON J., *Undergoing God*, p.29.
6   ALISON J., *Undergoing God*, p.30.

social projection. The question is not whether much of our God-talk is like this, but whether there is God-talk which is of a genuinely other Other. Following Alison, I have given two reasons for thinking that there is the possibility of monotheism which is not just our idea but is a confession arising from genuine encounter —confession arising from being addressed. We see such a discovery emerging over time in the Hebrew Scriptures as God ceases to be one of the gods. God is discovered to be far less interested in propping up Israel's identity over against the wicked other than in calling Israel itself to faithfulness through self-criticism. And God is discovered as knowable only insofar as the group gives up its own sense of what it already is and of who God is, and allows itself to be given being and identity through responsiveness to God's call. The group is a function of this God who remains «other» rather than the reverse. And that is why there is a sense in which this God is known as «hidden», just out of full view, never ours to control or possess.

Alison indicates that this understanding of God as discovery is fundamentally a contemplative knowing, such that, he says, «monotheism without contemplation is dangerous»[7]. This is going to be important for us later, as we consider how God is present and is to be experienced in our time of crisis. For now, at the end of this preliminary exploration of the concept of God, I want to repeat the remark with which I began: God is much more like «nothing (no-thing) at all» than like «one of the gods». If that is true, then the notion that God will make everything turn out by, for example, «fixing» global warming or anything else seems to me idolatrous. Whatever experiencing God might be in crises like these, it won't look like the appearance of a magician. But before we are in a position to consider what an authentic experience of God might be, we need also to ask some questions about what we mean by «experience».

---

7  ALISON J., *Undergoing God*, p.17.

## 2
## *So, Experience*

What is it that we experience when we experience God? How do we know that it is *God* we are experiencing? When I was younger and searching for a way to make God «real» to me, I used to long for some kind of extraordinary «experience» that would prove to me that God was there. I don't think I ever asked myself exactly what kind of experience would count, but I assumed it would be dramatic, some kind of «zap» moment, like the moment of Paul's conversion on the way to Damascus or some kind of miraculous answer to prayer. It would be, I thought, a «spiritual» experience.

Part of John Main's passion for teaching the way of contemplative prayer was his conviction that it was a practice through which all people could come to know God first-hand, could come to know the living God in their own experience. He insisted that only those whose faith was enlivened by this first-hand knowledge were capable of transmitting its reality to others. «The church», he said, «can only proclaim what it is itself being, what it is in the process of experiencing». And yet, he was equally insistent that in meditation we are not to aim at or to expect any extraordinary «religious» or «spiritual» experiences. «Don't ask yourself, he wrote, "am I levitating?" or "am I seeing visions?" That has nothing to do with it and in fact if you are levitating or seeing visions it is more likely due to drinking too much soda water than to the Spirit!»[8]. Mostly, he said, meditation will feel as though nothing is happening —and if perchance something does happen, the best thing is to ignore it.

So how does John Main's appeal to experience as the necessary ground of authentic knowledge of God, relate to his consistent teaching that in the practice of meditation we must not seek for spiritual experiences, or cultivate particular inner states or feelings? Part of the answer lies in a deeper grasp of the concept of «experience» itself.

The German theologian Jurgen Moltmann has remarked that the concept of «experience» is one

8  MAIN J., *Word Made Flesh*,

of the least explained concepts in theology[9]. For our purposes, however, a useful distinction is between experience possessed or acquired, and experience undergone or suffered. Moltmann has suggested that our modern Western concept of experience tends to focus one-sidedly on «active» experiences, experiences that we possess, acquire or master. These are experiences that we can say we have *had,* that are closed or finished, and that are no longer present to us or are present only as something past, as memory[10]. It is this sense of experience which often seems to be assumed by those lists that go around on the internet —thirty things you should do before you are 30, or 50, or 70. This is life experience to be «acquired»— seeing the Taj Mahal, climbing Mt. Kilimanjaro, bungy jumping.

But, Moltmann says, there are also experiences that befall or happen to us, limit experiences that we do not master. Elemental experiences of life, love, grief and death might be for us events *in* the past, but they never *become* «past». They are con-

9  MOLTMANN J., *The Spirit of Life: A universal affirmation,* trans. Margaret Kohl (London: SCM Press, 1992), p.18.
10  MOLTMANN J., *The Spirit of Life,* pp.21-22.

tinually present to us[11]. We live with these experiences —they become our companions. Moltmann says that these elemental or primary experiences «happen to us», they overpower us «without our intending it, unexpectedly and suddenly».

> When something like this happens to us, the centre of the determining subject is not in us —in our consciousness or will: it is to be found in the event that «befalls» us, and in its source. The person who experiences is changed in the process of experiencing. So although in German one talks about «making» an experience, it is not I who «make» the experience. It is the experience that «makes» something of me. I perceive the external happening with my senses, and notice that it has brought about a change in my own self[12].

So experience may be understood in terms of discrete events and one-off occasions, things which one aims to have in order to make life and oneself more interesting; or it may be understood in terms of the happening of life to us, that which makes and

11  MOLTMANN J., *The Spirit of Life*, p.20.
12  MOLTMANN J., *The Spirit of Life*, pp.22-23.

shapes us as much as we choose, make and shape it. Moltmann's point, and John Main's, is that experience of God is essentially of this latter kind —it is not something that we have or contain, but is something in which we ourselves are had or contained. Experience of God befalls us as a reconfiguration of self, a coming to be centred in the Other.

So John Main says, what enables us to speak «first hand» of God, is not in the first instance a «zap» moment treasured in memory. He does not deny that such «experiences» in the sense of one-off events can happen. But, he insists, they are not to be sought for themselves and, by themselves, they are proof of nothing —in fact, he says, they may be simply a sign of poor digestion. He said:

> Our spiritual growth can never be seen as an *accumulation* of experiences, rather it is the *transcendence* of all experiences. What we so often call a memorable experience is first and foremost a memory. But in the eternal act of creation which is the life of the Trinitarian God everything is *now*[13]

13 JOHN MAIN, *The Present Christ: Further steps in meditation* (London: Darton, Longman and Todd, 1985), p.108.

And likewise Moltmann has said: «The experience of God is always a suffering of the God who is Other, and the experience of fundamental change in the relationship to that Other»[14]. It is not something that we have, but is rather our entry into a new pattern of life. It is true that this means that one's inner, felt experience of life also changes, but that is a by-product of the experience of God rather than its essence.

3

*Experiencing God*

The main point of what I have said so far has been to deconstruct what I take to be certain false conceptions of what we are talking about when we speak of experiencing God. I have argued that the right use of the word God in the Judaeo-Christian tradition involves grasping at a very deep level that God is not one of the gods, not a player in our schemes of power and meaning. The true God is

14 MOLTMANN J., *The Spirit of Life*, p.6.

an «other Other», in James Alison's *formulation,* known only as discovered or encountered rather than as an idea. And I have argued that the experience of this God is never something I have simply as part of my suite of interesting life-experiences, a pinch of spiritual spice to liven up my dull existence. Rather, the experience of God is an undergoing of this other Other, such that my whole life is reconfigured, reoriented, re-centred. This experience need not be sudden and dramatic and in fact mostly is not. It is a slow and patient work of love and grace, undertaken in us by God over time, often recognised only in retrospect. Meditation is one way to open our selves, to consent, to this slow and patient work.

In the next two meditations, I'll be focusing more directly on how the experience of being related to this God makes a difference in times of crisis. In the last part of this meditation, however, I want to explore in more depth two aspects of the experience of God who is no-thing, and to suggest how that experience is related to contemplative practice. The two aspects are those identified by Alison as those which authenticate the «otherness» of God —the sense that God first addresses and calls us (monotheism is a discovery) and the sense that that call is necessarily connected to self-criticism.

4

*Being called*

30    The narrative of call and response is pervasive in the Judaeo-Christian scriptures and tradition, from the lives of the Hebrew patriarchs to the lives of the saints. From the stories of Abraham to Moses, Isaiah to Jeremiah, and Mary to the apostles, God is depicted as breaking into experience by addressing human beings, becoming known by making himself known. The great Protestant theologian, Karl Barth insisted that it is only because God has revealed God's self to us that we know God at all. «Without revelation man (sic) does not know that there is a Lord, that he, man, has a Lord, and that God is this Lord. Through revelation he does know it» (CD, p.309).

Now it might seem as if the biblical narratives of call and response are just exceptional instances, the dramatic zap moments that I earlier said were not necessarily constitutive of authentic experience of God. If I have never been addressed like that, then does that just mean that a first-hand experience of God is not available to me? I want to suggest that these narratives are not fundamentally about spiritual pyrotechnics, and that we misread them if we think they are. Instead, they alert us to three things.

First, they are dramatisations of the truth that God is the God who addresses us. In Alison's terms, they make the theological point that the true God is not an idea we have but a reality we encounter or, perhaps even better, a reality who encounters us. In John's gospel Jesus says to the disciples, «You did not choose me but I chose you» (John 15.16). A mark of God's independence from our fantasies about God is, it seems to me, the consistent testimony of those called that they are not necessarily thrilled about it. The call of God is often to a life more dangerous, uncertain and frightening than the lives we attempt to secure for ourselves, and the response of those called is, many times, outright resistance[15]. The prophet Jeremiah writes, like St. Paul, of the «necessity» under which he labours: «O Lord, you have enticed me, and I was enticed; you have overpowered me, and you have prevailed. I have become a laughing stock all day long; everyone mocks me... If I say, "I will not mention him, or speak any more in his name", then within me there is something like a burning fire shut up in my bones; I am weary with holding it in, and I cannot» (Jer.20.7, 9).

32 In the newer Testament, as Canadian theologian Douglas John Hall has noticed, the misgivings of human beings about being brought too closely into the orbit of the living God are shown by the way in which «the kingdom of heaven is customarily depicted, poetically, as a great feast, a bounteous banquet —*from which, ironically, everyone wants to stay away*»[16]. The true God addresses us and our response goes by way, very often, of resistance.

The second point about at least some of these stories of call and response is that they indicate that

15  HALL D.J., *Bound and Free: A Theologian's Journey* (Minneapolis: Fortress Press, 2005), pp.4-6.
16  HALL D.J., *The Cross in Our Context: Jesus and the Suffering World* (Minneapolis: Fortress Press, 2003), p.101.

we need to *learn* to hear the voice of God or to recognise God's presence. It is not as though we can take for granted that we will recognise when it is that God addresses us. In the Hebrew scriptures, the story of Samuel vividly illustrates this truth. Samuel is serving the ageing prophet Eli, whose eyesight (significantly) «had begun to grow dim». Samuel is lying in the temple of the Lord where the ark, symbolising God's presence in Israel, was residing. The Lord calls out to Samuel, «Samuel, Samuel», and Samuel, thinking it is his master Eli calling, runs to him saying «Here I am, for you called me». Eli says that he did not call, and sends Samuel back to his bed. Again, the Lord calls, and again Samuel runs to Eli. A third time this happens and, the narrator tells us, «now Samuel did not yet know the Lord, and the word of the Lord had not yet been revealed to him» (1 Sam 3.7). At last, Eli perceives that it must be the Lord calling, and he instructs Samuel how he should answer if the Lord called again: «Speak, Lord, for your servant is listening»[17].

---

17  A similar dynamic of initial non-recognition or can be seen in the stories of Moses and the b Abraham and his guests at Mamre, and Jac Bethel.

The possibility of hearing the address of God is the stance of listening and receptivity. This stance is signified in the Scriptures again and again by the Hebrew word «Here am I». In the New Testament, according to Luke's gospel, the condition of God's incarnation in the person of Jesus is Mary's faithful receptivity to this word, this address of God: «Here am I, the servant of the Lord; let it be with me according to your word» (Luke 2.38). Without this stance, there is no recognising God —and from the point of view of the authors of the New Testament, the story they have to tell is in part the tragic story that God came to God's people and his people «knew him not» (John 1.11). It is significant that the stories of the appearances of the risen Jesus to his disciples partake of this same dynamic of recognition and non-recognition in a particularly intense form. Even after they have been with him all that time, it is *difficult* to recognise God.

The third point of these stories of call and response is that they dramatise the extent to which our identity becomes a function of the one who calls. Sometimes this is signalled very obviously by the change of name which follows directly from being addressed by God: Sarai becomes Sarah; Jacob becomes Israel; Israel becomes a people; Simon becomes Peter; Saul becomes Paul. Again, as emerged from our discussion of Alison's essay, the God who addresses us does not serve to legitimate or stabilise my existing identity, but rather destabilises it and calls me into a much more provisional, responsive kind of life. This is an existence whose truest identity is found as it undergoes being called into being by the Other, by God.

This is the essence of discipleship, following the call in such a way as to be given identity from it and not from familial, social or religious belonging. This, as Dietrich Bonhoeffer said, is a «costly» way and yet, paradoxically, is the route to one's own deepest reality and stability. According to John's gospel, many of those following Jesus turned back when confronted with some of his most «difficult» sayings, sayings that conflicted with their pre-existing religious identity and understanding. So Jesus asked the twelve, «"Do you also wish to go away?" Simon Peter answered him, "Lord, to whom can we go? You have the words of eternal life"». Peter was coming to source his life in responsiveness to the call of Jesus.

How is the experience of the God who addresses or calls us, who is difficult to recognise and who gives us identity as a function of our response —how is the experience of this God related to contemplative practice? Contemplation is a practice of becoming still enough, silent enough, open enough to «hear» the voice of the other Other. It is a practice of readiness and expectancy. «Here am I» is the expression of the contemplative stance —open, receptive and listening. «Here am I» is a surrendering of one's own agenda and one's prior conceptions about what is needful, even about what is good. In the practice of meditation, in the giving up of thoughts, feelings, plans (even good ones) and in the silent repetition of the mantra, we learn a radical non-possessiveness in relation to our selves, our notions of God, our desires. In the space that opens up, we find ourselves beginning to tune in, at first barely recognising the sound, to the Word that resonates in the silence. We find ourselves *addressed*, and addressed we *find* ourselves.

# 5
## *Self-criticism*

The second aspect of the experience of God who is no-thing is its necessary connection to self-criticism. As Alison emphasised in his essay, a striking feature of the emerging monotheism of the prophetic literature is the fact that the God of Israel inveighs far more severely against the sins of Israel than those of the nations. Those who assume that belief in God is always about rallying God to «my side» have not read Jeremiah, himself reluctantly responding to the demanding call of God, testifying passionately for God against God's complacent people: «Run to and fro through the streets of Jerusalem, look around and take note! Search its squares and see if you can find one person who acts justly and seeks truth —so that I may pardon Jerusalem. Although they say, "As the Lord lives", yet they swear falsely» (Jer 5.1-2). And so on. Those who assume that the experience of God must necessarily be «a comfort» to believers, that it will result in a warm fuzzy feeling the majority of the time, have not paid attention to the discomfort and anguish of the prophets, the agonised wrestling of the martyrs and the struggles with truth, authenticity and sacrifice undergone by countless ordinary people of faith.

I have so far followed Alison's description of this aspect of the experience of God as «self-criticism». This is right, I think, but it is liable to misunderstanding. The self-criticism in question is not to be conflated or confused with that carping little voice that beats many of us up so much of the time —the one that tells us we are not good enough, or not self-sacrificing enough, or not worthy of much. Strangely, although it has a critical form, I may be all too comfortable with that voice— it has its drawbacks, but I know where I am with it. I know what to expect of it and of myself in the light of it. Rather, the self-criticism that signals that it is God we are encountering (as opposed to our wounded egos) is transformative, leading to true repentance and not simply an endless cycle of self-denigration. The self-critical, or perhaps self-reflexive encounter with God occurs not through the carping voice but through the cracking open of my false self and the stripping of illusions, one of which might be the carping little voice with which I am all too familiar.

Absolutely central to encounter with the God who is no-thing, then, is this process of stripping of illusions, of the false self and a process of allowing a truer, more authentic self to emerge. This is the process that the New Testament speaks of using metaphors of «dying to self», «leaving self behind» and «losing one's life in order to find it». Rowan Williams has said:

> Our healing lies in obedient acceptance of God's will; but this is no bland resignation. It is a change wrought by anguish, darkness and stripping. If we believe we can experience our healing without deepening our hurt, we have understood nothing of the roots of our faith[18].

It is important, again, not to mistake the metaphors. «Dying to self», «leaving self behind» are not the same as suppressing self to conform to

18 WILLIAMS R., *The Wound of Knowledge: Christian Spirituality from the New Testament to John of the Cross* (Cambridge, MA: Cowley Publications, 1990), p.20.

some pre-existing pattern of «goodness» or «right-eousness». Rather, it is about letting go of pride or self-image, letting our masks drop, being naked before God, inhabiting the vulnerability of our neediness, our fear, our anxiety, our imperfection. The death is the death of the ego that clings to a status of its own, that wants to secure its standing with or over against others, to possess a righteous-ness for itself. The death is the consent to humility and stripping, and for that very reason it is the con-sent to grace and gift. I receive as gift the self that I can never wholly seize or maintain by my striving.

Through the contemplative practice of silence and stillness, we consent to encounter this God who strips away our illusions, our false securities and false self-images. Even in our prayers and our spiritual disciplines we are often tempted to cover our nakedness with words, subtly justifying our-selves before God and others. In the daily disci-pline of contemplation, we are confronted directly with the vulnerability that we feel when we place ourselves wholly before God, relinquishing our excuses, withdrawing our projections and remov-ing our masks. It is the God we encounter in this hospitable place, whom we cannot but know as authentically Other.

6
*Conclusion*

∽

What is it that we experience when we experience God? How do we know that it is *God* we are experiencing? These are difficult questions to answer directly, but I have tried to indicate the direction we should be looking. The experience of God is rarely of *God* directly —indeed the Hebrew scriptures testify consistently to the danger of meeting God «face to face»— teaching that human beings cannot see God and live. The experience is rather of the reconfiguration of human lives in response to being addressed by an Other who simultaneously reveals and hides God's self. The experience is of undergoing transformation, remaking.

The experience of living life in response to this transforming address of God is, ultimately, of living from a deeper ground, tuned to deeper reality. The shape of this life is described in various ways in the witness of the Christian tradition —and in the third meditation, we will be looking in more detail at its contours and its connection to the practice of living contemplatively. But what I have emphasised in the last part of this meditation is that the journey to a life remade goes almost always by way of an unmaking, by the stripping or unmasking of our old identities, and by the call to a less settled, more provisional and responsive way of being. Such unmaking can be a painful process, where old certainties and structures of meaning no longer suffice or ring true. It is experienced often as the collapse of the stories we live by, and is mediated very often by a period of crisis. This is the theme of our next meditation.

*Meditation 2*

*Collapsing Stories*

## 1
*A Time of Crisis*

The language of crisis abounds in our culture. In my country, Australia —one of the world's most stable and ordered democracies— we face «crises» on at least a weekly basis. There are crises of leadership, crises of transport arrangements, crises of law and order, crises in aged care and health, and so on. According to media reports, celebrities face crises in their relationships almost as regularly and, so it seems, does the royal family.

In Middle English, so the Oxford English Dictionary tells me, a «crisis» was the turning point in the progression of an illness —the point at which the patient would either recover or die. In the Greek, *krisis* is the word for decision or judgement. In a sense we face little «crises» all the time and so it may be that our media are etymologically entitled to use the language of crisis to refer to any challenge or point of decision in public or private life. Nevertheless, if we think of crisis as the turning point between life and death, then to call most of what the news cycle calls «crisis» seems overblown —because whatever is the outcome of most of these decisions or upsets, the basic shape of the world will be the same after it as before. Not every decision, not every difficult experience is a crisis in the deeper sense that I want to use this word. Most of our decisions and experiences, even the more difficult or painful ones, are contained within an existing framework of meaning, on the same plane as life as we know it now. The world we inhabit, the perspective we have after such decisions and experiences is essentially the same as the one we knew before. The basic ground of our being and the meaning of our existence are not at stake.

The biblical story of Job can help us to see the difference between a painful experience and a crisis as I am defining it. In the first round of his misfortunes, all Job's livestock and his children are killed and yet, despite the severity of these losses, he is able to interpret them within his existing framework of meaning, within the narrative of his life up till now. He said «Naked I came from my mother's womb, and naked I shall return there; the Lord gave, and the Lord has taken away; blessed be the name of the Lord». Job is then tested more deeply. He is inflicted with «loathsome sores» and he goes to sit among the ashes. His wife incites him to curse God yet still he refuses to «sin with his lips». «Shall we receive the good at the hand of God, and not the bad?» he says (2.10). His friends come to console him and, appalled at his suffering which was «very great», they sit together on the ground for seven days and seven nights. When Job speaks again it is no longer possible for him to make sense of his life. «Job opened his mouth and cursed the day of his birth» (3.1). This is a full-blown crisis —it is not just that Job has suffered terrible grief and loss, but that the world he will inhabit after this time cannot and will not be the same. No matter to what extent his losses are recovered, this crisis will mark forever a turning point in his life, his sense of its meaning, his sense of its fragility. His life breaks at this point —it cannot be resumed on the same plane.

Crisis in the sense of there being a break or a deep rupture in our life, crisis in the sense of there being a before and a very different after, can befall us in many forms. My self, my sense of my past, present and future, can be called into question by the death of a spouse or partner, a parent or child, by divorce or the ending of a relationship, by the loss of reputation, by the loss of a life's work or of faith, by the onset of illness or dementia, depression or anxiety, by exile from culture and homeland, by the overwhelming trauma of war, torture or natural disaster, by many other occasions of loss and fear. Crisis can also befall us in the shape of a new and undreamt of possibility—the invitation into a new relationship, the discovery of a deeper, truer vocation, the call to relinquish old plans or dreams. On these occasions too, there is a turning point, a time of trial, discernment and judgement, a before and after.

In crises of all these kinds, we face two distinct forms of suffering. On the one hand, there is the suffering of whatever has befallen us in forms such as grief, terror, pain, loneliness, uncertainty, deprivation, shame or injustice. On the other hand, and this is what makes it a crisis and not only a difficult experience, there is the suffering created by the collapse of meaning, by the loss of the story we knew and were able to tell of our lives. I thought my life was amounting to this, but now that has gone. Who am I, now that my marriage has ended, my child has left home, my job has disappeared, my faith has become empty, my body is breaking down? Who am I now that my fears are overwhelming me? Some huge thing has ruptured my life, there is now a great gaping wound, and shards of point and purpose lie useless and broken around me. How can this ever be made whole again? How can this catastrophe be integrated into my life, especially since it seems to have disintegrated the very self who could have made any sense of it? The distinctive suffering of crisis is the felt impossibility, the despair of ever integrating what has happened into a coherent story, into a self and life whose narrative is collapsing.

And yet, if we are unable to integrate what has happened at least to some extent, then although a crisis may be survived or endured it will continue to dominate and define our lives. At the personal level, an enduring image of non-integration is the figure of the aged and bitter Miss Haversham in Charles Dickens's, *Great Expectations*, who lived her entire life in her wedding dress, frozen at the moment of crisis when she was jilted at the altar. Communities too can be unable or unwilling to integrate the trauma of crisis and so continue to be dominated by that moment. The bitter rehearsal of wrongs suffered hundreds of years ago as justification for present national or communal priorities testifies to that possibility.

So crisis is indeed, as the Chinese character suggests, a dangerous opportunity. It is dangerous because, if the crisis is profound enough, either we may be lost in an abyss of meaninglessness or despair, or the trauma of a time of crisis may remain a source of bitter poison for our lives and the lives of others. It is an opportunity because the re-integration of the life of a self or community and the rediscovery of meaning in the wake of crisis can never happen at the same level as before. It cannot occur merely as restoration. Re-integration, where it occurs after crisis, brings to birth a deeper wholeness and a truer relationship with reality which can be profoundly liberating and enriching. In this meditation, I want to ask how the contemplative experience of God in a time of crisis might lead us into that deeper wholeness and truth. To begin engaging this question, I will recap briefly some of

what we have discussed concerning our understanding of God.

## 2
*God and Crisis*
&

I spoke about the need to distinguish between
idolatrous and non-idolatrous use of the word
«God». I suggested that God is an idol to the extent
that «he» is a projection of group or personal identity, functioning to guarantee my/our security or
righteousness over against others. Following the
English theologian James Alison, I argued that God
is known and named truly only to the extent that we
encounter God as Other to all our projects and
schemes of meaning. This God is the God who addresses us and so is discovered rather than invented.
What is the evidence for the reality of God in this
sense?

Alison points out two things accompanying the
emergence of monotheistic confession in the Hebrew scriptures which are evidence that the God
to which they testify is genuinely Other. First, en-

counter with this God leads immediately to self-reflection and criticism. Whereas the god who is a function of group identity props up a righteous «we» against a wicked «they», the one God of Israel inveighs far more severely against the «we» whose God he is. This God calls Israel again and again to repentance and self-criticism, and convicts it again and again of this insidious form of idolatry and false worship. As I said, this is not just a matter of Yahweh's anger when Israel turns aside to worship the Baals, but perhaps more deeply of Yahweh's anger when Israel treats Yahweh as an idol: «I desire steadfast love and not sacrifice, the knowledge of God rather than burnt offerings» (Hosea 6.6).

And second, whereas the idol that functions to bolster group identity gets its identity from the group, in the monotheism of the Hebrew scriptures, it is Israel whose identity is given by God. Israel or the prophets are called into their true being through their encounter with God. And this God becomes known only as Israel or the prophets give up their sense of who they already are, and allow themselves to be given being and identity through responsiveness to God's call. In other words, the one called is a function of the God who remains «other» rather than the reverse. That is why there is a sense in which this God is known as «hidden», just out of full view, never ours to possess. And this means, likewise, that the life of those given identity through relationship to this God is much more responsive, much less self-possessed, than the lives we might set up for ourselves. Which again is why, as we saw, the initial response of many of those encountered by this God in the Scriptures is outright resistance. As Canadian theologian Douglas John Hall remarks: «in the newer Testament the kingdom of heaven is customarily depicted, poetically, as a great feast, a bounteous banquet —*from which, ironically, everyone wants to stay away*»[1].

All of this has implications for what it might mean for us to experience God in a time of crisis and for how such an experience might lead us into a deeper wholeness. I want to explore a number of lines of thought in this regard.

1   HALL D.J., *The Cross in Our Context: Jesus and the Suffering World* (Minneapolis: Fortress Press, 2003), p.101.

First, crisis is not foreign to God and to authentic experience of God. An idolatrous picture tends to assume that God is there to make the world and my life stable and safe. Worship, on this view, is about keeping God on side and crisis or catastrophe is a sign that God is not with us, or that we have fallen away from God[2]. On that picture, crisis and God are opposed to each other. I have been arguing against that theology. Indeed, if encountering the God who is genuinely Other leads to self-criticism and being called into a new identity, then (I am suggesting) it is very often encounter with God which *precipitates* or is precipitated by a time of crisis in human lives.

I want to forestall two possible misunderstandings of this claim. First, as I said, the self-criticism at issue in our encounter with God is not the carping little voice that besets many of us with self-doubt or a sense of unworthiness, or which keeps many of us locked in attempts at self-justification. Although that voice has a critical form, I may be all too comfortable with its agenda. What is at

2  See COWDELL S., «Christian Reflection on a Summer of Disaster», 2011.

issue in the self-critical encounter with God is rather the stripping of illusions, and strategies of self-justification and self-protection. It is, as it was for Israel, the process of coming to see the whole truth of ourselves, and the ways in which our untruth (including the carping little voice) damages both ourselves and others.

But this brings us to a second possible misunderstanding. One of the more offensive forms of religious discourse is the attempt to explain catastrophic events either in terms of God's punishment or of God's seeking to call those affected to repentance or to a deeper faith. I am arguing in this meditation that through a time of crisis we may indeed enter more deeply into the reality of our own lives and there encounter the reality of God more truthfully. But it is utterly illegitimate to make from there the explanatory move that God must have caused or willed the precipitating crisis in the first place. That again is to think of God as one of the gods, an idol, an explanatory cause in a system of meaning of *our* making.

It would take another meditation to deal in detail with this question, and it is true that there are ways of speaking about God in the Scriptures which make this explanatory move. But I think it can be shown in the emerging monotheism of the Hebrew bible and in the narrative of Jesus that the true God is uncoupled from this picture of a sovereign deity, master manipulator of events. Rather, the God revealed by Jesus Christ and the prophets is the one who enters and transforms human suffering and the abyss of meaninglessness from *within*. Douglas John Hall writes: «the message of the cross» is that pain and death «may only be overcome from within, not from above. And therefore the faith that emanates from this cross is a faith that enables its disciples to follow the crucified God into the heart of the world's darkness, into the very kingdom of death, and to look for light that shines *in* the darkness»[3]. God, in this conception, is not an *explanation* for suffering but meets us in the midst of suffering, suffering with us.

I have been speaking, then, of the way in which crisis is not foreign to God or our encounter with God. But what is it about a time of crisis that opens

---

3   HALL D.J., *The Cross in our Context*, p.32.

the possibility of being led into a deeper wholeness and truthfulness? It is, I suggest, that crisis reveals where our lives were lived at some level in illusion. This may seem more palatable to say of some crises than others. For example, in a crisis occasioned by the loss of reputation or even the ending of a relationship, I may come to see that my sense of myself or my expectations for the future were grounded in illusory or shallow soil. This need not mean that I was actively deceiving myself or that I was in any way insincere. It may just mean that, as things turned out, I was mistaken about reality. The crisis revealed to me a fuller truth about the way things were all along. But what about crises occasioned by the death of a loved one or by a calamitous natural disaster? Is it true to say that crises of these kinds reveal that our lives had been lived at some level in illusion?

Here it might be helpful to return to the distinction I made earlier between a crisis and a painful experience. I said then that the distinctive suffering of crisis is the collapse of the framework or narrative which could have made sense of the experience we are undergoing. Isak Dineson wrote that all sorrows can be borne if they can be put into a story. The suffering of crisis involves not only the pain of loss, grief or fear, but also the collapse of the story which might have helped us to bear it. In a tragedy as overwhelming as the recent Japanese disaster, or in catastrophic assaults such as torture or wrongful imprisonment, it is not surprising that any story we have told of our lives up till that point collapses. Such things are perhaps not containable within the scope of ordinary human stories, which involve assumptions about the usual rhythms of the natural world, the usual forms of human relating. That is what puts such events on the outer edge of what it is possible to integrate into the lives of communities and individuals.

And yet, such events do happen and may be experienced by us. And if in the face of them the narrative of our lives collapses, it is revealed that that narrative, that framework of meaning, was at some level illusory. At the critical moment it was found wanting, and proved insufficient for the reality with which it must now contend. There is no question of blame here—no question that the narrative «ought» to have been different all along. But what it means is that any re-integration of our story must come from a deeper ground. It must be able not only to help us to make sense of the new reality of our lives, but also to account in some way for what was lacking in the old story. It must be able to sustain us in making the transition from the person I was then to the person I am yet to become in the wake of this crisis. Without that, then my past cannot be brought into my new present. It is not integrated and given back to me, but is left behind. But if that happens then I am somehow left a fugitive in my own life, disconnected from my own history and so, disconnected from part of reality. As Rowan Williams has written: «The refusal or denial of memory is... dimunition, perhaps the deepest dimunition of all. If the whole self is the concern and theatre of God's saving work, then the past of the self must be included in the scope of this work»[4].

What then is needed? What might sustain us in the transition from the suffering of crisis into a deeper wholeness and truthfulness?

4  WILLIAMS R., *Resurrection: Interpreting the Easter Gospel*, revised edition (Cleveland: Pilgrim Press, 2002), p.23.

## 3
### The Wayless Way

In profound crisis, we can lose a sense of who we are and of where we are. Few if any of the old markers apply. The mystics speak of this place as the void or the abyss, and of the way that leads through it as the «wayless way». There is no new story that we can just decide to adopt in this place —for who is it that would adopt it? There is no map that we can follow from this place— for where are we and where is it that we would go? The image of pilgrimage may be helpful here. In a pilgrimage the pilgrim and the destination create each other. Although a pilgrim route has a destination, where you arrive at the end of a pilgrimage is, at some level, not specifiable in advance. And although it is the pilgrim who makes the journey, on the course of the journey the pilgrim is also made. So it is on the journey through the abyss. The destination towards which the pilgrim walks is wholeness, but the shape of that wholeness is not specifiable and does not exist in advance. It is knowable and it is realised only in the making of the journey.

To make this pilgrimage, to travel this way-less way, we need something that will help us to keep walking, to trust that there is indeed a «way» through even though, from where we begin, we cannot see it or imagine its end. In what follows, I want to suggest that the contemplative practice of meditation sustains us on and for this journey. In articulating its stages, I will draw on the Christian story of how God in the person of Jesus undertook this way through the abyss, and was accompanied by the Spirit. This is the story of the Triduum —the three days from Good Friday to Easter Sunday. The practice of meditation mirrors this story and (I believe) will lead us on the same journey. In this sense the practice of meditation will take us through a time of crisis regardless of our tradition. But this story also testifies, as I believe, that the journey is indeed possible, as well as naming the reality that sustains us in and through it. In this way, it creates the faith required to continue with the journey in the darkness of unknowing. And it provides, besides, a powerful se-

ries of images by which to bear its suffering and
negotiate the way.

4

## The Surrender of Friday

❧

A time of crisis befalls us. Usually we do not choose
it, and mostly we would avoid it if we could. Yet we
can choose to give ourselves to the crisis or resist it.
When Jesus was on the point of being betrayed by
Judas, as the community he had called into fellowship was in the process of collapse, he had to choose
whether to give himself to the abyss or resist. It was
an agonising choice. «Father, if you are willing, re-
move this cup from me; yet, not my will but yours
be done» (Luke 22.42). But by the time the soldiers
came for him, he could go to meet them: «See, the
hour is at hand … Get up, let us be going. See, my
betrayer is at hand» (Matt 26.45b-46). Giving ourselves into a crisis and resigning ourselves to the
inevitable are not the same thing. In our consent
there is the possibility of transformation, of creativity. For Jesus, that possibility took flesh in the

symbolic enactment of communion in the face of the disintegration of his community. As the Dominican theologian Timothy Radcliffe has written of the institution of the Last Supper:

> Jesus did not just make any sign. It was a creative and transforming act. He was to be handed over into the hands of his enemies. He would be entrusted by one of his own disciples into the brutal power of the Empire. He did not just passively accept this: he transformed it into a moment of grace. He made his betrayal into a moment of gift. He said, «So you will hand me over and run away; I grasp this infidelity and make of it a gift of myself to you»[5].

It might seem that the choice to consent or resist applies only to those crises that, like Jesus's, were foreseeable. What about those crises that befall us utterly unawares —the sudden death of a loved one, a violent assault, the annihilating force of a tsunami? In what sense might we consent to these appalling ruptures in our lives? It is true that in crisis the precipitating event may be utterly independent of our will and our control. Whether we consent or not, it has happened. But there is still a question about whether we consent to be in the place it leaves us, or whether we resist. As long as we resist, we may have the illusion of maintaining some control. We may have the illusion that we can go back to where we were. Yet as long as we resist, then we cannot begin the journey through. We can only start the journey of integrating the catastrophe that has befallen us from where we now are, from the place of being overwhelmed and stripped of what formerly had held the story of our lives together.

The practice of meditation assists us in surrendering the stories we live by. In that sense it pre-empts the moment of crisis. If we have been meditating before crisis hits, we may find ourselves able to dwell amidst the collapse of our stories with less anxiety than we otherwise might. If we begin to meditate in the midst of crisis, we are helped gradually to consent to be where we are. We are helped to let go of the story that has sustained us until now. How does meditation enable us to make this surrender?

In the tradition of meditation handed on from Father John Main, we are prepared in this way through the practice of saying the mantra. When I began seriously practising meditation, I would often experience a sense almost of vertigo. This wasn't so much a physical sensation as a psychological and mental one. It was something like a deep resistance to keeping my attention on the prayer word, the mantra, and an almost overwhelming compulsion to come back into my thoughts, into the familiarity of my interior monologue. Refusing that monologue, I felt vulnerable and exposed. I realised that my sense of self was constructed out of that continuous stream of thoughts and feelings, and the sub-conscious interweaving of these into the story I told of my life. Without them, who was I? Where was I? What would become of me?

John Main was very clear that the practice of meditation is a practice of leaving self behind, of dying to self. This is not the moralistic and often violent form of self-denial preached by certain forms of Christianity. It is rather the surrendering of the whole self to God, which means surrendering our self-consciousness and the stories through which we maintain our identity over time. John Main wrote in his first book on meditation:

> It requires nerve to become really quiet. To learn just to say the mantra and turn away from all thought requires courage… Meditation is the prayer of faith, because we have to leave ourselves behind before the Other appears and with no pre-packaged guarantee that He will appear. The essence of poverty consists in this risk of annihilation[6].

He went on to say that:

> There comes a delicate moment in our progress when we begin to understand the totality of the commitment involved in self-surrendering prayer, when we see the total poverty involved in the mantra[7].

6   MAIN J., *Word into Silence* (London: Darton, Longman and Todd, 1980), p.23.
7   MAIN J., *Word into Silence* (London: Darton, Longman and Todd, 1980), p.23.

This movement of prayer corresponds to the complete surrender of Jesus, handed over to death with no pre-packaged guarantee of resurrection. How does it help at a time of crisis? It gives us a practice by which we can consent to be where we find ourselves, in a story-less space. It gives us a place from which to begin the journey. We do not yet know how the journey out of the abyss is possible, or that there will be any new meaning or any solid ground. In meditation, all we do is to consent to begin the journey in faith. The new self and the new story that will emerge on the other side of this surrender is not something that we will construct or of which we are in control. It will be of a different order to the self and the story we are in the process of leaving behind.

5

*The Waiting of Saturday*

After the acute moment of crisis on Friday, comes the interminable waiting of Saturday. And again there are no guarantees. In his magisterial theology of Holy Saturday, Alan Lewis notes that although the story of Easter is three days, the centre of the drama, Saturday, is an empty space: «between the crucifying and the raising there is interposed a brief, inert void: a non-event surely —only a time of waiting in which nothing of significance occurs and of which there is little to be said»[8]. Or is it he asks, after all, «a *significant* zero, a *pregnant* emptiness, a silent nothing which says *everything*»[9].

After the crisis of Friday and the collapse of that story, there is a space, an interval. In that interval the old story no longer has any meaning or makes any sense, but there is no new story to tell. It is often the interval after a crisis which feels impossible to bear. In the tradition, Saturday is the day of the descent into hell. Lewis speaks of the «eerie, restless day of burial and waiting... perhaps for nothing»[10]. How long will this empty time last? Will time ever not be empty again? The impulse to resolve the tension, to fill the space, is overwhelming. Hold-

---

8  LEWIS A.E., *Between Cross & Resurrection: A Theology of Holy Saturday* (Grand Rapids, MI: Eerdmans, 2001), p.1.
9  LEWIS A.E., *Between Cross & Resurrection*, p.3.
10  LEWIS A.E., *Between Cross & Resurrection*, p.5.

ing our nerve through the time of Saturday teaches us the meaning of hope. The theologian Jurgen Moltmann has distinguished authentic hope from the premature closure of despair, on the one hand, and presumption on the other hand. Authentic hope is vulnerable and waiting. It might not know what the gift of new life will look like, but it refuses to be satisfied with counterfeit forms. Simone Weil wrote that when someone is hungry it does not matter whether they believe that there is bread; all that matters is that they do not, by a lie, convince themselves that they are not hungry.

How is this Saturday time transformative? How is it a necessary stage in the journey to deeper wholeness and truthfulness in the aftermath of crisis? I want to suggest two sides to the significance of this time. First, it is significant that what has been surrendered to death is really dead. Speaking theologically of Jesus's journey, Saturday means that God enters into the reality of death and overcomes it, as Hall puts it, «from *within*». Death is not a place unknown to God which means that not even death can separate us ultimately from the God who is prepared to suffer death with us. Speaking of our journey through crisis, Saturday is the space in which our old story, our old self is given time to loose its hold on us (or perhaps, it is the space in which we are given time to loose our hold on it). It may be that on Friday we suffered the death of a framework of meaning, a life held together in particular ways, but the scaffolding of those frameworks and the grief of their loss can exert power over us for some considerable time. Saturday is the space where what has died is allowed to be buried. It becomes the soil in which the possibility of the genuinely new might germinate.

And second, Saturday signifies that the new life that arises, though contiguous with our previous life is also not something latent or dormant in what has died. The new life is from the future, not the past. Speaking again theologically, it is significant that in the resurrection narratives, the power to rise from the dead is not within Jesus, for Jesus is dead. It is in the power of the Spirit, by the power of God, that Jesus is raised. The resurrected life is gratuitous —it is received as gift. In the journey through crisis, the emergence of new life is also experienced as gift. The timing is not at our behest and, even more significantly, the new life is not ours as possession. I will say more about this in a moment.

The practice of meditation is a practice in which we learn to give ourselves to this Saturday time and to trust the space. We learn to live without our old story, and not to scramble too quickly to adopt a new one. We learn not to panic as life seems to be slipping past with no clear direction or certainty of resolution. Mostly, John Main said, meditation will feel as though nothing is happening. Say your mantra and keep saying your mantra. As we do so, we learn to trust that the space of having no story is in fact habitable, and that —like the desert, like the tomb, it may yet be filled with possibility.

6
*The Gift of Sunday*
ﾟﾉﾉﾟ

After a time of profound crisis, we do not resume our lives on the same plane. That is not just because the old stories no longer suffice to hold the meaning of our lives, but also because we recognise the fragility of all stories, of all the certainties which scaffold but never fully insulate our lives. We realise that, in an instant, everything can change and that all we have depended upon for our sense of ourselves and our meaning may be swept away. Unintegrated or resisted, that realisation can become a source of crippling anxiety or despair. Integrated, I want to suggest, it makes possible the kind of lightness of being we associate with some of the saints, a non-defensive and non-possessive demeanour in the face of the vulnerability of life. How is that so?

I think there are two reasons for that. First, we do not emerge from the collapse of our stories, brand new, as if nothing had happened. The resurrected Jesus bore on his hands and feet the scars of his crucifixion. It is the whole of Jesus's life, including his death, which is taken up into his resurrection life. What is significant about this is not simply that he bears the scars of his death as we might bear the scars of our past hurts. It is that the new life is bigger than and is not ruled by the power of death. Death no longer has dominion over him, as Paul puts it. For Jesus there is a freedom in relation to death that was simply not available before. And something similar is possible for us.

Say the crisis I have suffered is the loss of my reputation. And say I gradually emerge from this crisis, having been on a long journey of letting go my investment in what others think, my attachment to my legacy, my sense of shame and humiliation. If genuinely new life (as opposed to a reconstructed or rehabilitated life) arises for me on the other side of that journey, my relationship to my reputation will be forever changed. My concern for my good reputation will never have the power over me that it once did. I will have a freedom in relation to what others think of me, that I could never have had before. In the practice of meditation, I have entered the abyss of this loss and found it habitable. I have received the gift of a new life bigger than the life I have lost.

Second and relatedly, the life that follows the death, the new story we become able to tell, never becomes another solid possession, a fixed meaning. We know now that none of this belongs to us securely. Its gift character continues and it calls us into an ever deepening pilgrimage of dispossession. When Mary Magdalene recognises the resurrected Jesus, he says to her «Do not hold onto me»,

«Do not cling». In the resurrection narratives, Jesus is always ahead of the disciples —calling them to meet him in Galilee, sending them into the world. At one level, this feels a more vulnerable, precarious kind of existence. But at another level, it is a life increasingly at peace and at rest. We are no longer seeking to secure our own meaning or safety. We receive our lives and our meaning as gift and adventure rather than desperately trying to defend ourselves against a hostile fortune. The experience of crisis dispossesses us, ready or not, of aspects of our lives. In the practice of meditation we consent to this movement and we learn to live in the liberating dynamic of dispossession. We are taught to hold on less tightly to the lives and the meanings we create, which means that our lives are grounded evermore deeply in reality, in what actually is, as opposed to what we say should be. And in the end, this is experienced as the relief of living in truth.

### 7
## Conclusion

Much of what I have said has focused on the experience of the individual in crisis, and how contemplative experience of God helps us to integrate that experience into a deeper wholeness and truthfulness. One striking feature of this journey is that as we are stripped of our stories and the meanings we cling to so tenaciously, we begin to know ourselves as sharing in the vulnerability of the whole creation. We are pressed into the common ground of our creatureliness. We experience our kinship in grace and mortality[11]. Loosening our attachment to the identities we have constructed for ourselves begins to overcome the illusion of our separateness. This experience resonates with John Main's pro-

---

11 James Alison speaks of the movement of letting go self-justification insofar as we receive being forgiven, acknowledging our complicity in systems of violence and exclusion. This movement, too, as he says leads us into being steadily more at home with being «ordinary», one of the «crude mass» of humanity. *Knowing Jesus* (Springfield, IL: Templegate Publishers, 1994), pp. 93, 100.

found understanding that the practice of meditation creates community. The more we can let go of ourselves, the less defensive and self-protective we become, the more we are present to and rejoice in the sharedness of our humanity. As we let go of ourselves, we are freed to love and attend to the particularity of other people.

This means, then, that the deeper wholeness we can come to experience in the wake of crisis is not just an individual wholeness or reintegration, but is the experience of our deeper relatedness to all that is. We belong much more consciously to the community of suffering humanity and to the community of creation. And what this means, in turn, is that our deepening wholeness is not just for ourselves, but contributes to the coming into wholeness, the reconciliation, of all things. Through overcoming our personal dis-integration and alienation, we are able to realise (in both senses of that word) what Thomas Merton called the «hidden wholeness» which underlies all that seems separated and alienated. We become signs and agents of reconciliation for others. So in the same way that Jesus's life and death and resurrection could be given back to his disciples in such a way that fuller communion with God and with humanity was made possible, so our lives, brought into deeper wholeness through the costly pilgrimage through crisis, may become an offering for the healing of the world.

# *Living Contemplatively in a Time of Crisis*

## 1

*Grace*

∽

Thomas Merton tells a famous story of the moment he realised his communion with the whole human race.

> In Louisville, at the corner of Fourth and Walnut, in the center of the shopping district, I was suddenly overwhelmed with the realization that I loved all those people, that they were mine and I theirs, that we could not be alien to one another even though we were total strangers. It was like waking from a dream of separateness, of spurious self-isolation in a special world, the world of renunciation and supposed holiness… This sense of liberation from an illusory difference was such a relief and such a joy to me that I almost laughed out loud. And I suppose my happiness could have taken form in the words: «Thank God, thank God that I *am* like other men, that I am only a man among others»[1].

---

[1] MERTON T., *Conjectures of a Guilty Bystander* (Tunbridge Wells: Burns & Oates, 1995), pp.156-157.

Part of Merton's liberation was from the illusion that, as a monk and a solitary, he was somehow «a different species of being», a «pseudoangel», *better* than others. And yet, he realised too that it was because of his solitude that he had come to this point of clarity. He wrote:

> This changes nothing in the sense and value of my solitude, for it is in fact the function of solitude to make one realize such things with a clarity that would be impossible to anyone completely immersed in other cares ...[2].

For this reason, he sees his solitude as undertaken in some way «for others», to keep this realisation alive.

> My solitude... is not my own, for I see now how much it belongs to them —and that I have a responsibility for it in their regard, not just in my own. It is because I am one with them that I owe it to them to be alone, and when I am alone they are not «they»

2 MERTON T., *Conjectures of a Guilty Bystander*, p.158.

but my own self. There are no strangers! Then it was
as if I suddenly saw the secret beauty of their hearts,
…the person that each one is in God's eyes. If only
they could all see themselves as they really *are*. If only
we could see each other that way all the time[3].

I have known a similar kind of experience
—perhaps some of you have too. I suspect it is not
such an uncommon experience as we might think.
Mine came after a time of prolonged crisis in my
life, where I had been teetering on the brink of what
felt like a catastrophic failure, battling anxiety and
a terrifying sense of being suspended over the abyss.
The prospect of this failure put me in touch with
the realisation that my sense of my own value had
been tied up with a felt need to become «someone»,
and that to justify my existence I needed to con-
tribute more to the world than others. For other
people (I realised I had assumed), it might be
enough to live an «ordinary» life, to have an ordinary job and ambitions, but that was not enough
for me. I had to make a difference. Stripped of the

---

3  MERTON T., *Conjectures of a Guilty Bystander*, p.158.

sense that I was going to be capable of making that difference, my life felt like something shameful, something that I would just have to survive.

My salvation came sitting on the edge of Darling Harbour, in Sydney. Wrestling with this deep fear and sense of inadequacy, I realised that I was never going to be able to make myself adequate in my own eyes. But for the first time I realised that no one apart from me was saying that I needed to be more than everyone else just in order to be enough. I finally realised that I could not justify myself and, even more amazingly, that I did not have to. I could just let myself be... here... The relief of that liberating moment was indescribable. Finally I could relax and rejoice in being simply a human being among others, no better and no worse. Like Merton, I found myself laughing out loud, delighting in being absurdly, wonderfully, simply human. Like Merton, I awakened to a profound love of others —a profound compassion for all of us. At the time, I was working in the Senate of the Australian Parliament doing research for Senate Committees. Soon after this experience I was in a Committee meeting, and overwhelmed by the wonder and beauty of a rather obnoxious Senator from Western Australia. As Merton wrote:

> As if the sorrows and stupidities of the human condition could overwhelm me, now I realize what we all are. And if only everybody could realise this! But it cannot be explained. There is no way of telling people that they are all walking around shining like the sun[4].

Contemplation and crisis can each take us to this kind of place, the place that Iris Murdoch calls «unselfing». Here it is not that we are consciously unselfish, or nobly self-forgetful; it is simply that we no longer have an ego capable of propping itself up or seeking to keep itself separate. In my experience, the grace of crisis was that it took me to a place I would never have gone willingly, a place where I saw as illusory the means by which I had been attempting, all my life, to secure myself in the world. I had been defeated by the thought of starting that project again. There was no energy left for self-

4  MERTON T., *Conjectures of a Guilty Bystander*, p.157.

making. That realisation could, and did for a while, lead to despair. But once I realised not only that I *could* not remake myself but that mercifully I *did not have to*, I entered the realm of grace. I entered the place where I could receive as gift that which I had striven all my life to earn as achievement, a sense of being at home with myself, with others and with reality.

I explored in some depth features of the way through the experience of crisis which are also features of the contemplative journey. This is a way which, regardless of our tradition, can help us travel from the terror of the collapse into meaninglessness and isolation to the joy of communion and love. I drew on the Christian story of the three days from Good Friday to Easter Sunday in order to articulate stages of this pilgrimage. I spoke of the surrender of Friday in which we consent to let go of old ways of making life secure or understanding life's meaning; the waiting of Saturday where we wait in an empty space, between the collapse of our previous stories and the emergence of a more truthful story; and finally, the gift of Sunday where we receive new life in such a way that our past and present is integrated into a new future. This new life is never simply on the same plane as the life we surrendered. It is both wounded and healed —bearing the scars of what it has suffered, but also freer of old limits and fears and filled with new graces.

There is nothing automatic or glib about this progression from death to resurrection. There is unhealed suffering in the world; there are crises from which people do not appear to «recover». There may be different reasons for that. Sometimes, we are not willing to let go of an old story or to wait for the new one to emerge. Sometimes, perhaps, people do not find the resources or the teaching or the companionship they need to begin the journey through. Sometimes a crisis is so deeply damaging of self, that the work of integration is still incomplete at the end of a lifetime; there is a sense in which this is true for all of us. It is part of the testimony of faith in the Judaeo-Christian tradition that the cry from the broken heart will always find a response in God, but that does not mean that the journey is quick or easy. For this reason, consenting to embark on the pilgrimage through crisis always involves risk and trust. It is the same with the pilgrimage of contemplation. John Main said:

> It requires nerve to become really quiet. To learn just to say the mantra and turn away from all thought requires courage… Meditation is the prayer of faith, because we have to leave ourselves behind before the Other appears and with no pre-packaged guarantee that He will appear. The essence of poverty consists in this risk of annihilation[5].

Most of us begin the pilgrimage through crisis only when there is no alternative. We know we cannot go back to our old way of being with our old frameworks of meaning. They have failed and been shown to be illusory. The only way to new life is through the crisis, consenting to poverty and risking annihilation. It is no surprise then that the life that follows this death and the new story we become able to tell never again becomes a solid possession. We know in the wake of the experience of crisis and renewal that none of this belongs to us securely.

5   MAIN J., *Word into Silence* (London: Darton, Longman and Todd, 1980), p.23.

What this means is that the three day journey of surrender, waiting and gift is made not just once in our lives, but becomes a way of life. Even after a time of acute crisis has passed, we are always in the place of being invited to enter more deeply into reality and into truth. And this movement always involves a letting go, an emptying, and an opening to new life. Contemplative prayer is the means by which we can live our whole lives as this pilgrimage.

In the story that Merton tells and in my own experience, a striking feature of this journey is that we begin to know ourselves as sharing in the vulnerability of the whole creation. We are pressed into the common ground of our creatureliness and we lose the illusion of our separateness. This means that the deeper wholeness we enter in the wake of crisis and through contemplative practice is not just a strengthened individuality, but is the experience of our deeper relatedness with all that is. We belong much more consciously to the community of humanity and creation in all their beauty, joy and suffering. And this means, in turn, that our deepening wholeness is not just for ourselves, but contributes to the coming into wholeness, the reconciliation, of all things.

The paradox then of both the contemplative life and a time of crisis is that by taking us deeply into our selves, meeting and learning to accept whatever is painful, unresolved, or illusory within us, we are empowered to move back into the world with a radically deepened sense of connection. We find ourselves living with a new freedom and courage, with a heightened spirit of adventure, hope and joy. In this meditation I want to open up for our discussion how this deepening inner pilgrimage frees us to be more wholly and vitally in the world. I am going to focus on three interrelated ways in which our experience of life is different: our relationship to death; living in the «tragic gap»; and moving beyond being right. In all three of these dimensions, I suggest, living contemplatively transforms our experience of being alive and expands our capacity to become agents of liberation and healing for others.

*Living Until We Die*

౼౿

«Karl Barth said that Mozart's music was so powerful because it contained a great No, swallowed
up in a triumphant Yes»[6]. The crises of our lives are,
in a sense, great «no's». They interrupt our plans,
our loves and our identities. They also put us in
touch with «no's» that we may not have realised
were within us. Resistance, avoidance, denial, re-
sentment, illusion, fear. I have been exploring how
contemplative practice can help us to be with and
enter into these great «no's» so as to be brought by
a greater «yes» into fuller life. This exploration has
so far focused on the crises that occur *within* the
course of our lives —loss of a loved one, a job, reputation. There is a sense, however, in which our
whole lives are lived in the shadow of the final crisis of death. And this crisis is not one from which
we will emerge into new and fuller life, at least not
in the sense we have been exploring so far. We will

6  RADCLIFFE T., *What is the Point of Being a Christian?* (London: Burns & Oates, 2005), p.20.

not emerge from this final crisis into new life, because we will be dead. What difference does it make to live contemplatively in the shadow of death?

This is an important question because our relationship to the final crisis of death deeply affects how we live. This truth has long been recognised by the spiritual traditions of the world. If the prospect of our death is not integrated into our lives then, whether we are aware of it or not, death runs our lives. Death, in St Paul's words, has dominion over us. There are some pretty obvious features of our culture that seem utterly bound by death and the fear of death —our obsession with youthfulness, our fear of losing our looks, our anxiety about accumulating possessions, our culture of obsessive risk aversion and insurance, the gating away of the disabled and infirm whose presence makes denial more difficult. The aggression of individuals, groups and nation states, too, the assumption that «I'd better get you before you get me» seems connected to a pervasive fear of death and non-being. And tragically, the escalation in depression and suicide particularly among young people seems to indicate, not a freedom in relation to death, but death's colonising of life in the forms of despair and meaninglessness.

How might we begin to integrate the crisis of death into our lives? How might we free ourselves from being covertly run, in one way or another, by death? I said just now that the crisis of death is not one from which we will emerge into new and fuller life, at least not in the sense we have been exploring so far. The temptation of Christian discourse has been, at times, to deny that. We don't need to worry about death, really, because death is just the gateway to eternal life. There is a sense in which I believe this, but I am concerned if it is offered too glibly as a «solution». As Rowan Williams has said:

> The weightiest criticisms of Christian speech and practice amount to this: that Christian language actually fails to transform the world's meaning because it neglects or trivialises or evades aspects of the human.

One of the ways in which it does this is to risk «being unserious about death when it speaks too glibly and confidently about eternal life»[7]. Timothy Radcliffe has protested against the Christian form of avoiding the reality of death by way of easy piety:

> If we do not endure sorrow and even anger, then we shall not be able to mourn. Faced with death, we should be desolate. There is a prayer for the dead, frequently and incorrectly attributed to Bede Jarrett OP, which claims that «death is only an horizon, and an horizon is nothing save the limit of our sight». And one wants to protest. It appears to trivialize death, as no more dramatic than a trip to London. Henry Scott Holland did not even think that he was going that far: «Death is nothing at all. I have only slipped into the next room»[8].

We will die and nothing is served by denying that reality. And yet, whether or not we feel able to say that we «believe in the resurrection» and in the ultimate triumph of life over the power of death, it

7 WILLIAMS R., «The Judgement of the World» in *On Christian Theology*, Blackwell, Oxford, 2000, pp.29-43, p.40.
8 RADCLIFFE T., *What is the Point of Being a Christian?*, p.84.

seems to me that contemplative practice helps us to journey towards death more openly and non-defensively. How does it do this? By inducting us in the surrender of our lives as we know them, it is enabling us to lean into the unknown and, through the experience of many little gifts of new life along the way, teaching us to trust in possibilities from the future, possibilities beyond our control. As we learn to live contemplatively, trusting our lives to this dynamic of surrender, waiting and receiving, we grow in faith that this is the truth about how reality works. And if this is how reality works in life, then the death we die and the reality into which we die, need not be totally alien to us. We may have no real sense of what this will look or feel like, but to the extent that we can journey towards this final crisis non-defensively and non-anxiously, our lives are freed *now* for living.

Of course, this is a matter of faith. But this does not mean that we need to try very hard to believe something we are not sure we can believe. It is a matter of faith in the same way that our response to any crisis is a matter of faith. Either we take the risk of entrusting ourselves to the unknown, facing our fears and resistances, our «no's» —or we don't. If we take the risk of trust, we don't know for sure how we will emerge on the other side. But if we don't take this risk then it is the crisis that will end up defining and confining our lives.

How is life different if we are able at least to begin the work of integrating the final crisis of death? I find this a challenging question. I think, for me, it means being more prepared to respond to life as an adventure. I will say more about this later, but maybe I don't have to be so anxious about passing milestones that our culture tells me I need to be ticking off —married by a certain age, children, a certain kind of house, a certain retirement plan. Maybe being free of the dominion of death is about trusting the unfolding of my life, trusting the integrity of my journey, and being less concerned with comparing myself to where other people are up to.

As we get older, being free of the dominion of death could look like continuing to live as openly and fully as we can in old age, rather than pulling up stumps early in anticipation of the end of the game. I recently heard a wonderful story about a woman, Mary Ann Schaffer, who had always wanted to write a novel, but who had never got around to it. Finally, in her 70s, she began. She finished her book and though she never saw it published, she knew before she died in 2008 that it would be published in 13 countries. It is called *The Guernsey Literary and Potato Peel Pie Society* and it became a best seller. The point is not that it became a best-seller, but that at 70 she still had a book in her and she let it out. Mary Ann Schaffer is someone who did not let the proximity of her death stop her from living in the meantime. She lived right up until she died.

Our lives with each other could be very different too. As James Alison has pointed out, it is fear of death which often dominates our relationships. We avoid all that smacks of non-being or that threatens vulnerability. This shows up, he suggests, in patterns of rivalry and competition, always having to get ahead, insisting on rights, and not doing more than we have to[9]. It shows up in our fear of

---

9 ALISON J., *Knowing Jesus*, Templegate Publishers, Springfield IL, 1994, p.56.

being numbered among the victims of the world, and so we avoid solidarity with those liable to become victims. A potent sign of living free from the dominion of death is offered by those who remain in situations of violence or persecution for the sake of others. I think of Sister Dorothy Stang, murdered in Brazil in 2005 for her work with landless peasants to preserve the Amazon rainforest from illegal logging. I think of Aung San Suu Kyi risking her life for the freedom of the Burmese people. I think too, of those who are willing to be with the outcast of our societies, overcoming the fear of contagion by association and offering friendship to those despised or liable to become victims of mob violence; those who work with the mentally ill or the drug addicted, those who work with asylum seekers, those who work with prisoners and paedophiles.

Living contemplatively towards the crisis of our mortality sets us free *for* life, and *from* the dominion of death. It sets us free to live fully right up until we die and to share our lives non-defensively with and for the sake of others. As we engage in this greater solidarity with the life and needs of the

world, however, we can be overwhelmed —by the
scale of the world's suffering, by the seeming fu-
tility of our efforts to make a difference— overwhelmed by the pain of living in what Parker
Palmer calls «tragic gap».

### 3
*Living in the Tragic Gap*
∞

Reflecting on his own struggle in and with this
gap, Parker Palmer writes of spending time with
the Catholic worker movement in New York in the
1960s. Members of this community lived among
the poor of the city, advocating for them with
social services, picking up the pieces as they fell
through the cracks in the system time and again.
They ran a kitchen which provided for many of
these people the only meal they had each day. As
Palmer saw the endlessness of the need and the
endlessness of the task he asked one of the long-
term workers how she could continue. Wasn't it all
pointless? Wasn't it impossible to make a real difference? She replied, «Parker, just because some-

thing is impossible, it doesn't mean you shouldn't do it»[10].

Many might agree with this sentiment, and yet it seems a recipe for burn out. To give oneself to an infinite task, a bottomless pit of need, can be overwhelming. To be aware of the suffering that is and the healing that might be, and then be unable to bridge the gap… how can we stand to live our whole lives in this place? Of course, many can't and so they opt out. We might embark on lives of service, activism or social change, but many of us find ourselves at some point exhausted, resentful and disillusioned. And, speaking for myself, this experience played itself out in both a desire to avoid being confronted anymore with the suffering of the world and guilt about my avoidance.

Can living contemplatively make a difference to our experience of life in the tragic gap? I suggest that there are two forms of inauthentic relationship to the tragic gap that contemplative practice enables us to be liberated from. First, the gap is not about me. I spoke at the beginning of this talk of a

10  *The Active Life: A Spirituality of Work, Creativity and Caring* (San Francisco: Jossey Bass, 1990) p.76.

time when I felt that justifying my life required that I make some profound difference to the lives of others. It was not that my concern for others was false, and not that I do not have a contribution to make. The problem was failing to notice how much of my experience of the gap was tangled up with what was unresolved in me. Although my life was ostensibly about making a difference to others, at a deep level I was still at the centre of the picture. I was *using* the gap and my relationship to it as a way of trying to justify myself, to make myself whole. But when we make the gap about ourselves, then we have no freedom in our relationship to it.

At his inauguration as President of the new democratic South Africa, Nelson Mandela danced. I was very moved by his evident joy but also puzzled. I wondered how he could dance so freely when he knew what was ahead of him and when so much of the suffering of his country was unresolved. How could he be free in the face of all that? I wonder now if it was because, although he was absolutely committed to bridging the gap between what was and what might be, *his* wholeness and *his* freedom were not dependent on that work being accomplished. He was already free and indeed it was partly his inhabiting that freedom in advance of its fulfilment that announced and opened it as a possibility for others.

In a similar vein, Palmer has written of a friend who has lived with resolute fidelity to the cause of peacemaking, only to see an increase in wars and rumours of wars. «So how does he stay healthy and sane?» «How does he maintain a commitment to this sort of active life?», Palmer enquires. «His answer completes the koan offered by my friend at the Catholic Worker: "I have never asked myself if I was being effective, but only if I was being faithful". He judges his action, not by the results it gets, but by its fidelity to his own calling and identity»[11]. But paradoxically, when we live this way we do make a difference.

The second inauthentic form of relationship to the tragic gap is to think that our only options are either to ignore it or to fix it. Both of these ways of relating to the gap are violent and untruthful. This is brought out very clearly in a story that

11 PALMER, *The Active Life*, p.76.

Parker Palmer tells of his experiences of profound clinical depression. In this state, he said, he has suffered greatly from the responses of those who either could not be with him at all or who wanted only to make him better. But, Palmer says, the only person who really made a difference was the friend who found a way to be with him, alongside him in the darkness. This friend would simply massage Palmer's feet for a time each afternoon, rarely ever speaking. Palmer describes this as a way of being that was neither evasive nor invasive.

The practice of «being with», neither evading nor invading the integrity of others, is transformative. It is transformative in those situations that cannot be fixed —when someone is dying, or living with dementia, or suffering depression or profound grief. This is because it keeps the person suffering in fellowship with the rest of us. They are not left to suffer alone as if we can no longer bear to be present to them, and this means that they can continue to be present, less fearfully, to their own experience. And it is likewise transformative for those situations in which taking some of kind of action is a possibility. Action that arises from having attended deeply and non-compulsively to the reality of a situation is very different from the re-action driven by my anxiety to assert control and so deal with my helplessness and other unmet needs.

Contemplative practice forms us for «being with» reality, letting it and ourselves be. It enables us to discern more clearly when there is something to be done and when there is not. And it enables us to distinguish more clearly between our own needs and the needs of the world. As I am able increasingly to be with my own feelings, of frustration, grief and powerlessness, so I can be in situations that can't just be fixed at will with a greater measure of peace and freedom. Nelson Mandela could give himself to an endless work, because he was free in relation to it. And that meant he could enjoy its fruits as they ripened, even as others were snatched from the tree. Living contemplatively in the tragic gap opens the possibility of joy in the midst of sorrow and suffering, and of remaining there even when the prospects of «success» seem distant and uncertain.

*Beyond Being Right*

The third dimension of contemplative living that I want to explore is what I am calling moving «beyond being right». I have already touched on one aspect of this movement in the experience of letting go the project of self-justification. There are other aspects of this movement too which relate to broader questions about the nature of contemplative ethics. For now, I want to focus on how moving beyond the need to get our lives «right» frees us to be fully ourselves and to receive our lives, as it were, from the future.

Iris Murdoch said that it is sometimes hard to know in philosophy how much one is speaking about a general question, and how much one is working through one's own personal psychology. This may be a case of me mistaking a personal issue for a general one, but I want to suggest that it is a tendency in human cultures to map out the shape of a «good» or a «successful» life. The culture and individuals within it then measure their lives and the lives of others according to their conformity to the accepted pattern. There may be more than one pattern available, with variations allowed for by class, gender, ethnicity, place in the family, religious and political affiliation and so on.

In our culture, ostensibly, we are radically freer from these kinds of expectations than were previous generations —and it is true that we are freer to make our lives in accordance with our own choices than were most of our grandparents and great-grandparents. Nevertheless, our advertising and superannuation industries, not to mention religious and social groups, still assert a pretty strong picture of the «right» kind of life. At my middle class school, for example, the «right» life included university qualification, decent job, respectable marriage, family life, community involvement and solid retirement. For many of us, it seems to me, part of the suffering of crises such as divorce, discovering oneself to be gay, addiction, childlessness, and redundancy is being judged to have failed at life.

The problem with seeking to live the «right» kind of life, of whatever pattern, or in rebelling against it as teenagers are wont to do, is that it is based in abstractions and pays no attention to the particularities of our personality, history and context. This means two things. First, I may be trying to live a life that is not truthfully mine. And second, I buy into the illusion that my life is a matter of pure will rather than more deeply of call and response. Basing our lives on pre-set patterns, no matter how noble or worthwhile we believe these patterns to be, in the end does violence to ourselves and violence to the world.

As well as violating fundamental truths about ourselves, this way of relating to our lives closes us to possibility and to the contribution we may actually be called to make. Theologian Devin Singh makes a distinction between the concepts of «*futurum*» and «*adventus*», which helps to articulate this idea. *Futurum* assumes complete continuity between the present and some future point —we extrapolate from current conditions to depict what the future will and should be. By contrast, *adventus* is based on the possibility of something breaking into the system; «something radically other and new... comes to meet us, from the future, as it were»[12].

In the Judaeo-Christian tradition, God is a God who breaks in from the future and who calls people into the unknown. Importantly, although this call sometimes seems unlikely and unpredictable in the light of the past, it does not violate the basic nature of the person called. It is more that, when the stammering Moses is called to lead his people to freedom or the Christian persecuting Saul is called to preach the gospel to the Gentiles, God draws out and enlivens dimensions of their deepest self and possibility. This is a self and possibility so deeply hidden that they may never have become aware of it themselves had they not taken the risk of hearing and responding to God's call, a call that in these cases at least came in the context of crisis.

The Scriptures are full of stories of God's servants being asked to embark on a journey, or to undertake a task, or to live into a promise with no

12 SINGH D., «Resurrection as surplus and possibility: Moltmann and Ricoeur», *Scottish Journal of Theology* 61 (3): 251-269 (2008), p.260.

clear information about where to go, or how to do it or what the outcome will look like. Think of Abraham setting out from Ur, of Sarah laughing incredulously at the promise that she would bear a son, of Mary asked to be the mother of God, of Jesus driven into the desert. These were not ventures that conformed well to culturally let alone religiously approved expectations of a «good» life. Central here is the conviction that God can do a new thing if only we, having discerned the call and possibility, will give our lives to the risk of it. The future here is not defined in advance or by probabilities. The future breaks in as possibility and gift —open to the radically new, and able to be created from nothing.

Being open to and becoming agents of this kind of possibility and new life in the world requires the practice of deep listening. This is listening both to self and to the Other who calls, listening we are formed in by the daily practice of silence and of listening to the mantra. This kind of contemplative living from the future invites us to be less threatened by criticism and more open to live our truth; it asks us to practise discernment and courage as we risk following the call into the unknown. On this adventure, although our listening happens always in dialogue with community and with the wisdom of the tradition, we cannot finally delegate our responsibility for our lives to others or to patterns of the «good» life set down in advance. We are never assured of our «righteousness» absolutely. The cost of a living relationship with ourselves and with God is this risk of getting life or bits of it «wrong». But to refuse this risk is to refuse to live truthfully at all. Douglas John Hall has said:

> The whole purpose of faith is to free us for life —for full and actual daily living— and to illumine the meaning of what occurs to us, *not* to insulate us from all the confusing and negating dimensions of our finitude, but to give us the courage to enter more deeply into the unknown that is around us and within us[13].

---

13 HALL D.J., *The Cross in Our Context*, p. 28.

## 5

*Experiencing God in a Time of Crisis*

I have spoken of three interrelated dimensions in which living contemplatively in and through a time of crisis gradually transforms, almost without our knowing it, our experience of being alive and our capacity to become agents of liberation and healing for others. As we listen more deeply to our lives and respond more faithfully to the call upon them, we are freer from the dominion of death. Trusting in the integrity of our own journeys, we do not need to defend our lives so anxiously against the risk of non-being or of the unknown. We are released to take action for possibilities that call us and also from the need to justify ourselves by our works. As I said at the beginning, then, the paradox of the contemplative life and the experience of crisis is that by taking us more deeply into our selves, they send us back into the world with radically deepened capacity to be with and to love other people, to live non-anxiously in ways that offer wholeness and hope. St Seraphim of Sarov said: «Be at peace, and thousands around you will find salvation». The work we undertake towards healing and wholeness in ourselves is work that we undertake for the world.

This series of meditations has been called «Experiencing God in a Time of Crisis». I have spoken of the difference it makes to live contemplatively. More broadly, what I hope this has done is to throw light on the meaning of the word «God».

In the first meditation I spoke of the need to distinguish between idolatrous and non-idolatrous use of that language. I suggested that God is an idol to the extent that «he» is a projection of a group or personal identity, functioning to guarantee my security or our righteousness over against others. Following James Alison, I argued that God is known and named truly only to the extent that we encounter God as Other to all our projects and schemes of meaning and justification.

In the light of the discussion of the second and third meditations, I suggest that «God» is the name of the reality, the voice, the Other, whom we encounter in the place where we are stripped naked, brought by the experience of crisis and of contemplative prayer to what the tradition calls «poverty of spirit». It is here that we are sufficiently «unselfed» that the God who is not merely a function of our need and identity can pass through the walls of self-justification, self-assertion, self-protection and self-preoccupation which usually surround us. Life sourced in relationship to this Other is responsive, open, adventurous and at home with what is not yet fully known or resolved about its future or the future of its commitments. Despite experiences of suffering and grief, there is also a lightness and non-anxiousness born of wounds and dividedness integrated and accepted. The authentic experience of God in and through a time of crisis does not rescue us *from* our lives but makes them fully our own. In this way our lives become a gift to ourselves and to others, a sign of the possibility of wholeness in a broken world, a testimony to the ultimate reality of love and life.

*A beautiful and simple proposal to construct our Spiritual Life through Discernment and Prayer of the Heart*

One of the greatest experts in the spirituality of Eastern Christianity, Cardinal Špidlík, deals in this book with prayer and spiritual life, with the experience of grace and goodness, through discernment of evil and human passions in everyday experience. It is a beautiful and simple proposal to construct our spiritual life through discernment and prayer of the heart. ✍

*Tomáš Špidlík was born in Boskovice, now in the Czech Republic, in 1919. Špidlík is Professor of Eastern Spiritual Theology, and Cardinal, and is known as one of the greatest experts in Eastern Christianity today. He has been chosen «Man of the Year, 1990» and «the most admired person of the decade» by the* American Bibliographical Institute *of Raleigh in North Carolina.* ✍

*The Art of Purifying the Heart*
Tomáš Špidlík
isbn: 978-1-934996-18-8
112 Pages
Series Sapientia

## Is Life in Society Possible without Morality?

Sergio Bastianel answers the question by addressing the responsibility of Christians to confront issues of justice within society in ways that promote the common good. The author, places a priority on human relationships based on sharing and solidarity. He emphasizes the interconnections between personal morals and social justice and raises fundamental questions about such issues as political life and economics, about hunger and development, and about the true meaning of «charity», all of which are relevant issues in our contemporary societies.

Sergio Bastianel s.j. is currently professor of moral theology at the Pontifical Gregorian University in Rome and also serves as its academic vice-rector. He spent his early years teaching and lecturing at the Pontifical Theological Faculty of San Luigi in Naples, Italy, and in later years he served as dean of the theological faculty of the Pontifical Gregorian University.

*Morality in Social Life*
Sergio Bastianel
isbn: 978-1-934996-14-0
360 Pages
Series Episteme

*Experiencing God in a Time of Crisis*

This book was printed on *thin opaque smooth white Bible paper*, using the *Minion* and *Type Embellishments One* font families.

This edition was printed in D'VINNI, S.A., in Bogotá, Colombia, during the last weeks of the fourth month of year two thousand twelve.

*Ad publicam lucem datus mensis aprilis,*
*festivitatem Divina Misericordia*